Monito Hermoso

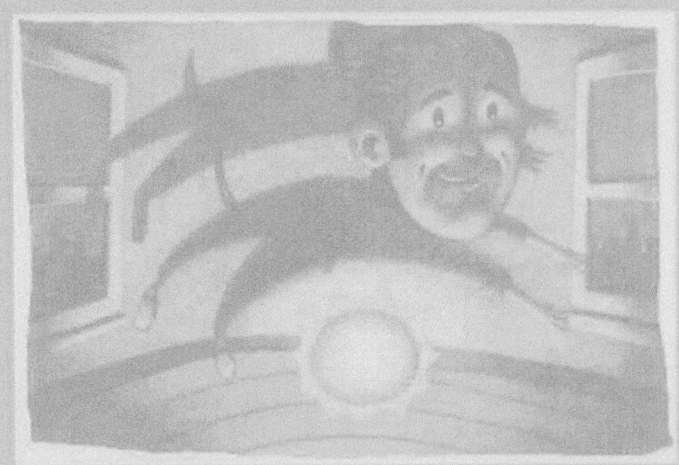

A collection of paintings
Volume One

~~~

Mike Cressy

www.mikecressy.com

~~~

Book Design/Publisher
JetPak Studio

Lovingly dedicated to the memory of
Holly McClure

"BeeZurk Butterfly"

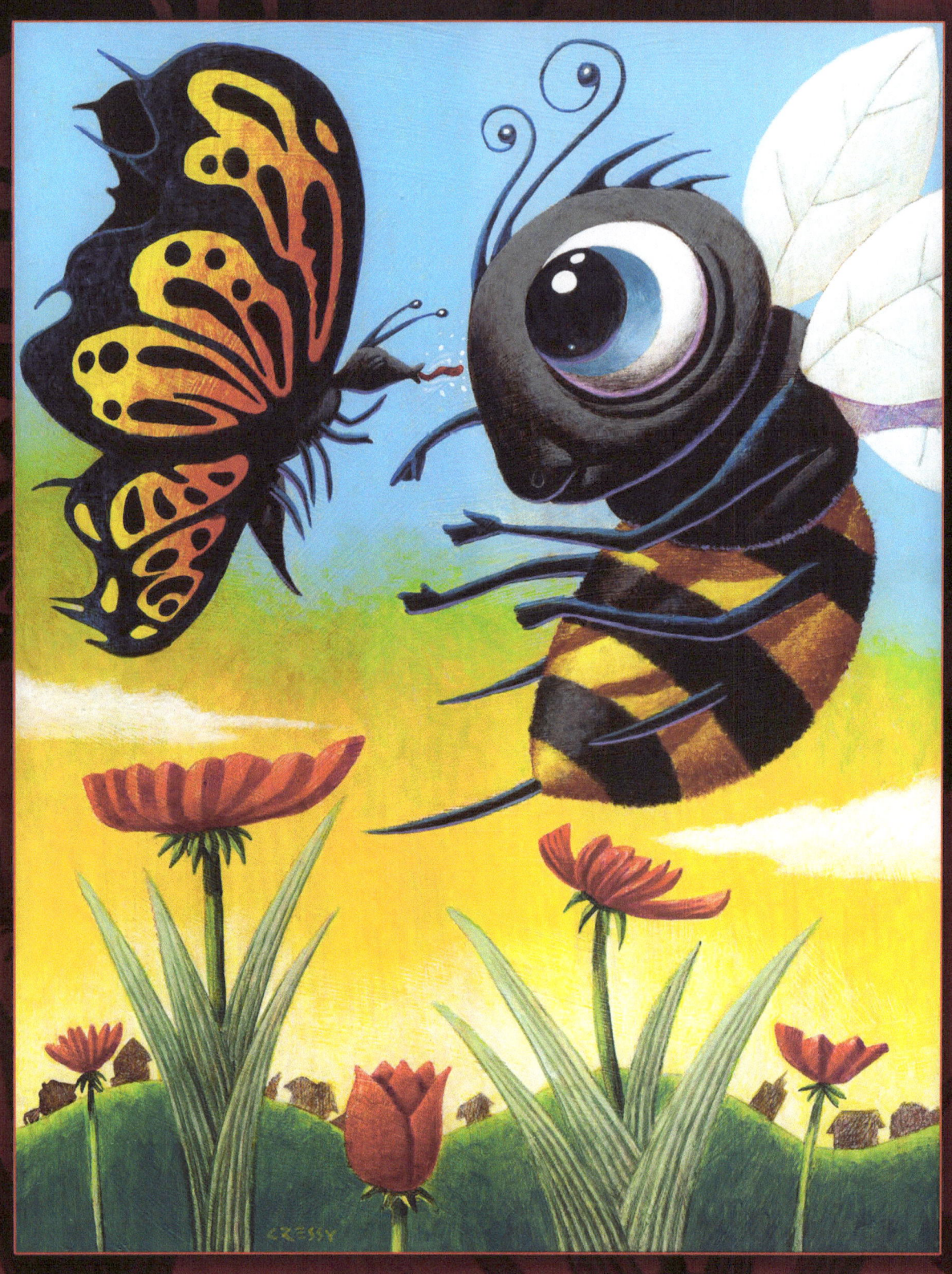

16" x 20" – Original Size

"The truth shall make you free,
but first it shall make you angry"

"ArizonA"

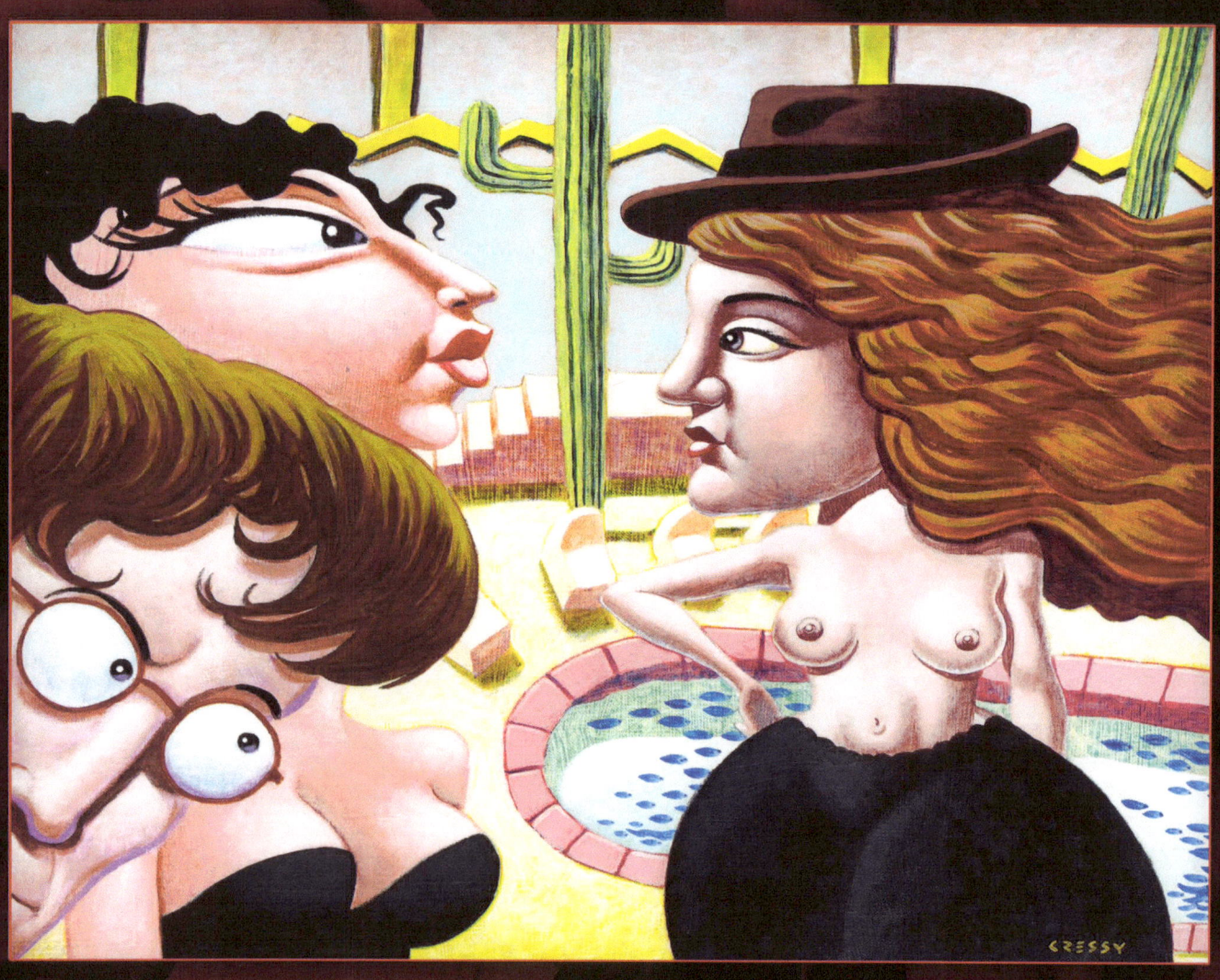

20" x 24" — Original Size

"The naked intellect is an
extraordinarily inaccurate instrument"

"Space Girl"

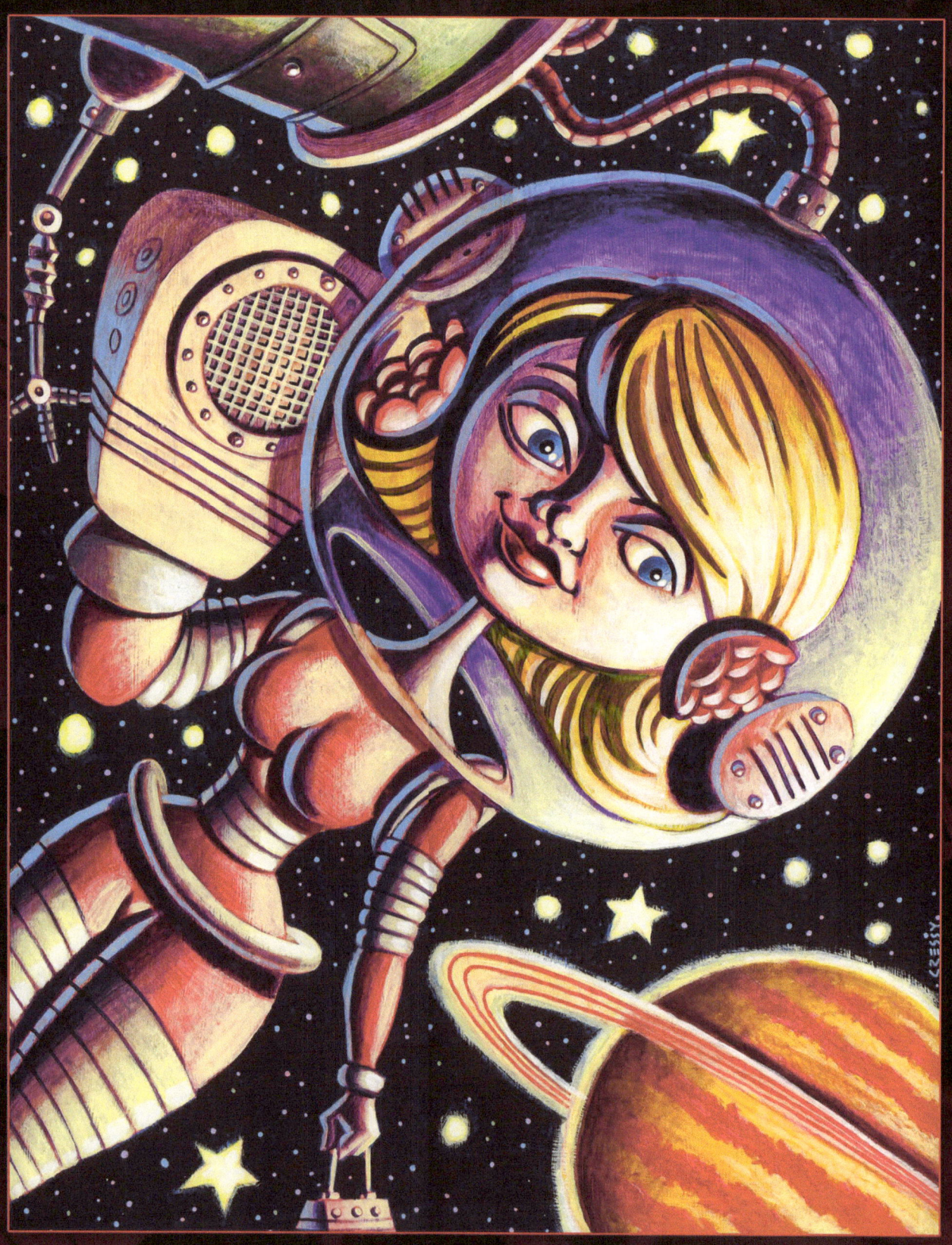

16" x 20" – Original Size

"If you take big paces you leave big spaces"

"The Three Amigos"

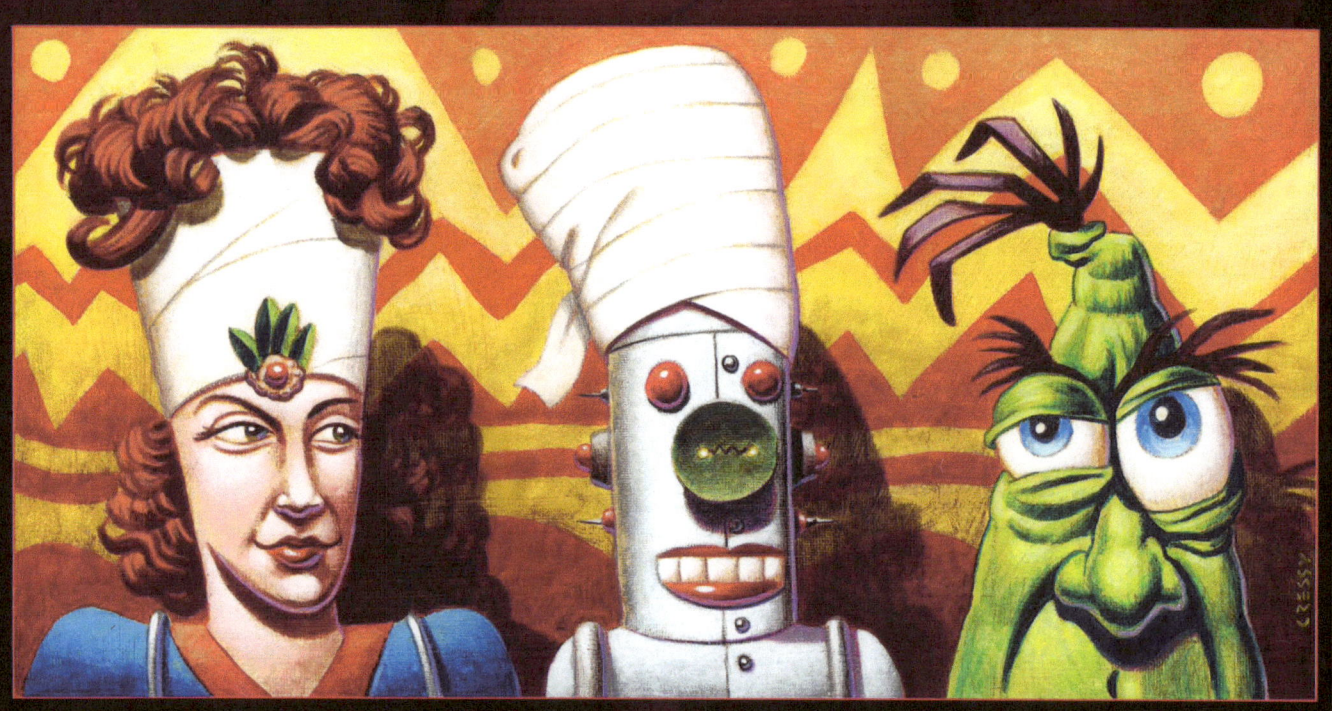

10" x 20" – Original Size

"Friends aren't jumper cables.
You don't throw them into the trunk
and pull them out for emergencies."

"Tiki Island"

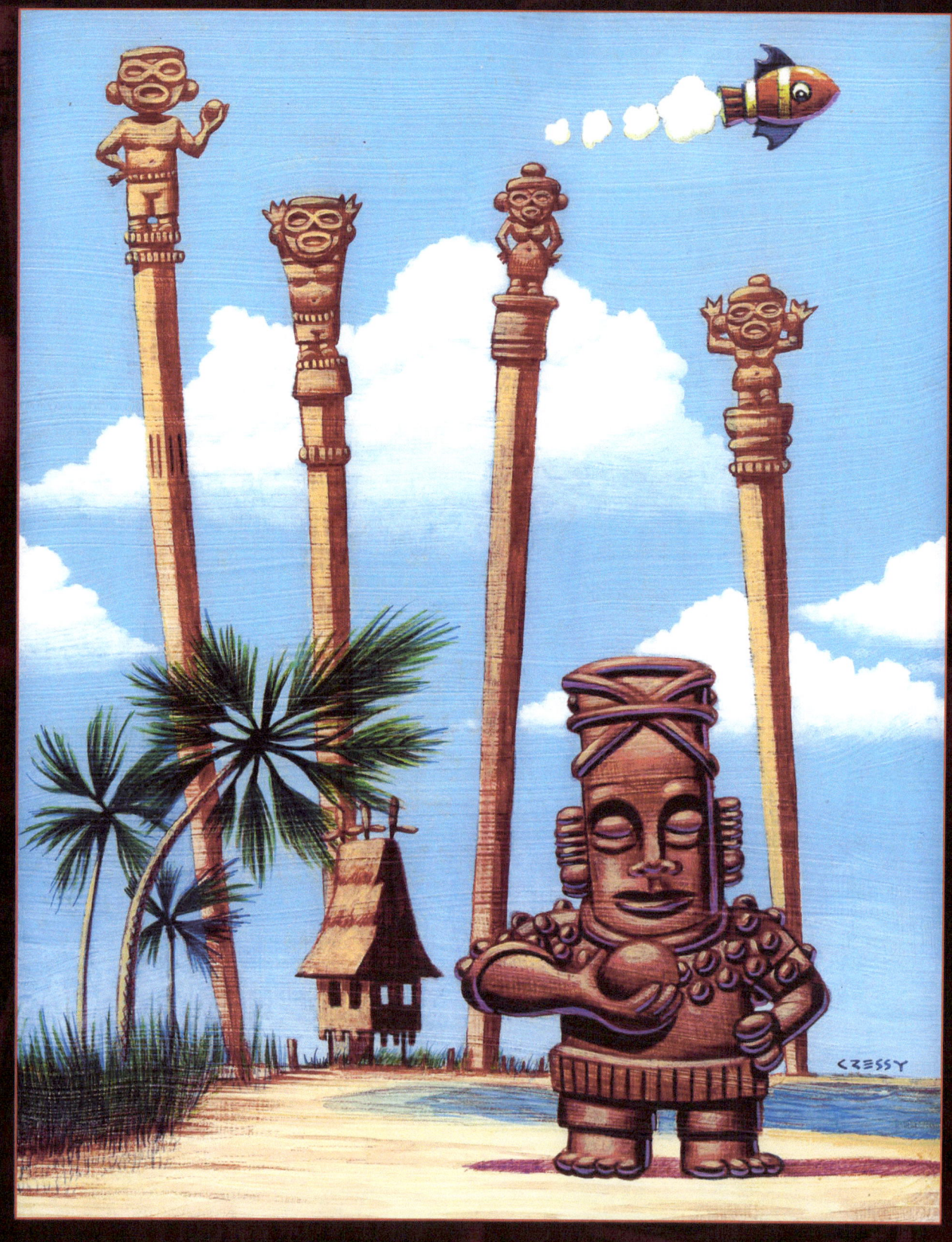

11" x 14" – Original Size

"Once again, I turn to the collective knowledge of Tiki Central:
OOOGA BOOGA!"

"Swingin' Cats at the Hep Cafe"

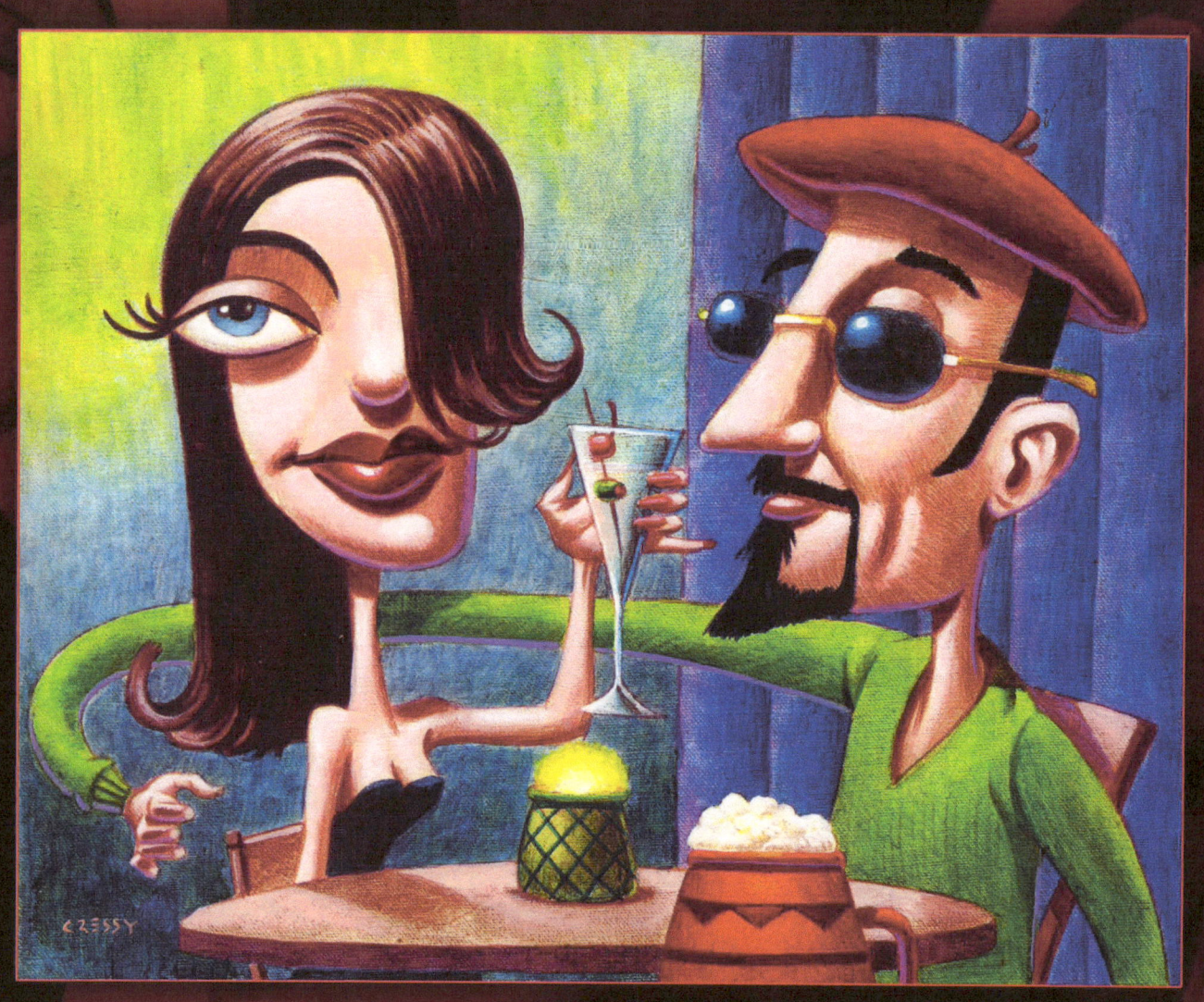

11" x 14" – Original Size

"I'm really diggin' this jaaaaZZ, maaan! This cat is really hip! Far out daddy—o!"

"Last Call AM"

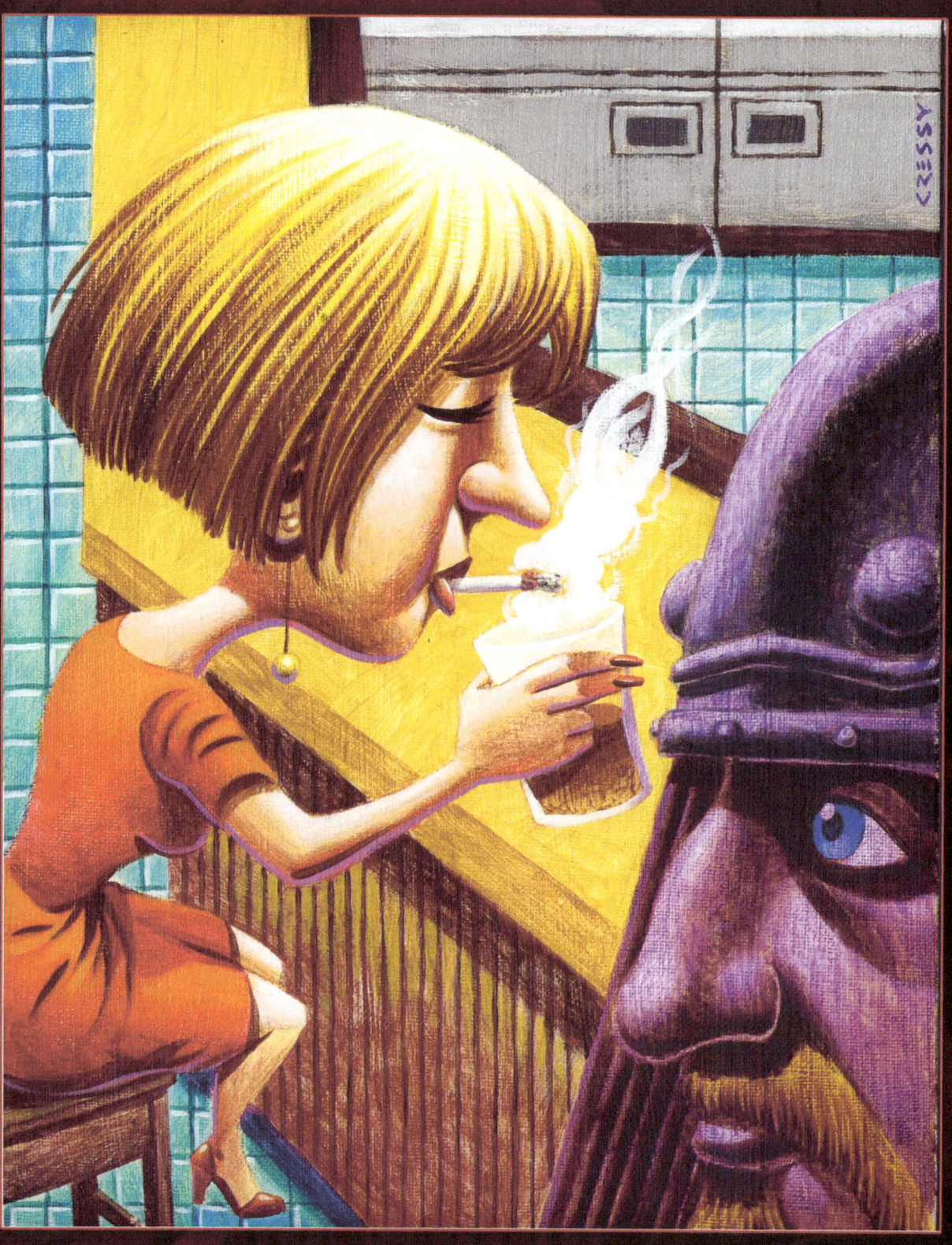

11" x 14" – Original Size

"And the bar tender says to
Renee Descartes:
"Another beer?" And Descartes says,
"I think not," and disappears"

"Apotheosis of Nihilism"

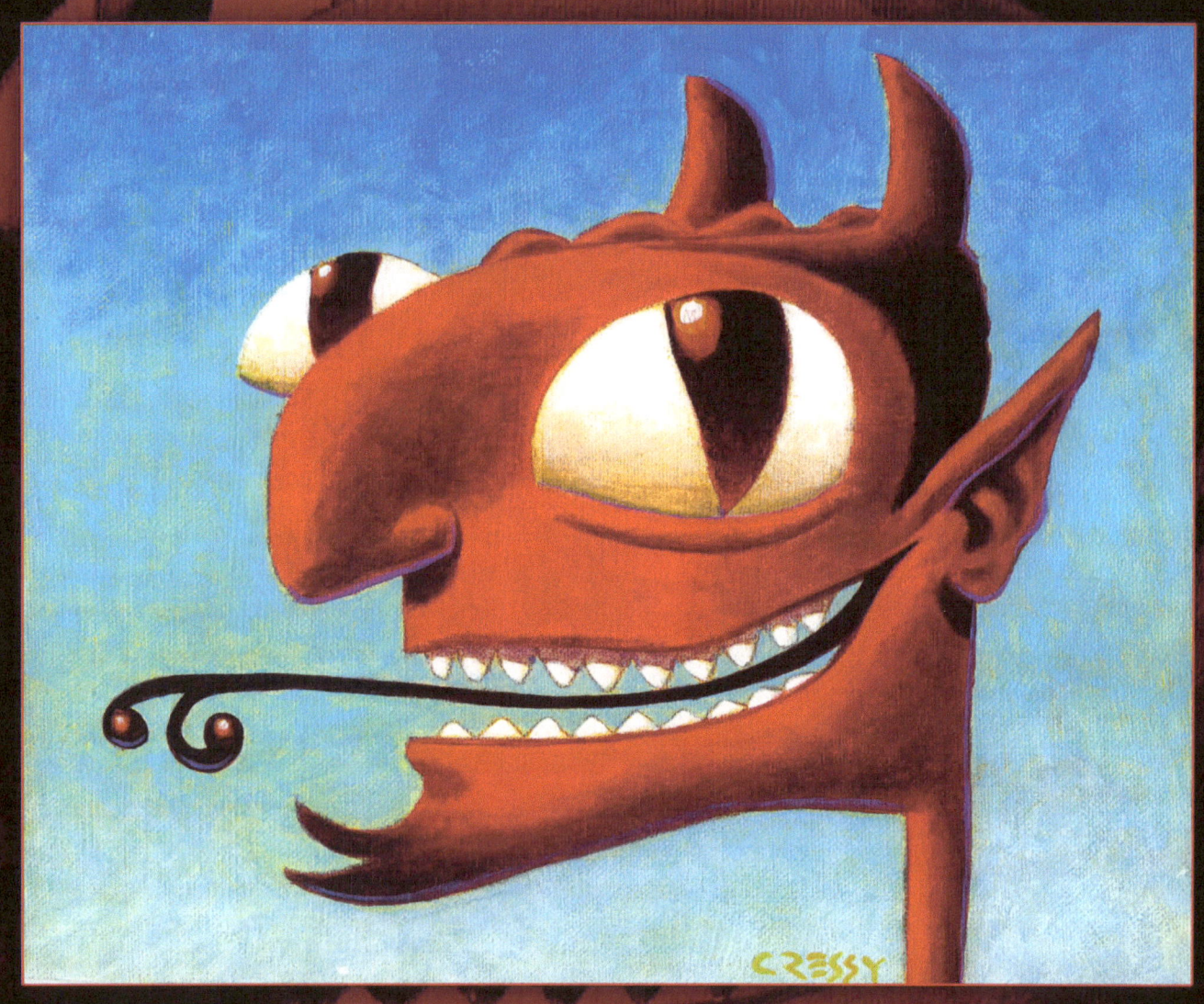

11" x 14" – Original Size

"A little greed
can get you lots of stuff."

"Golden Bowl"

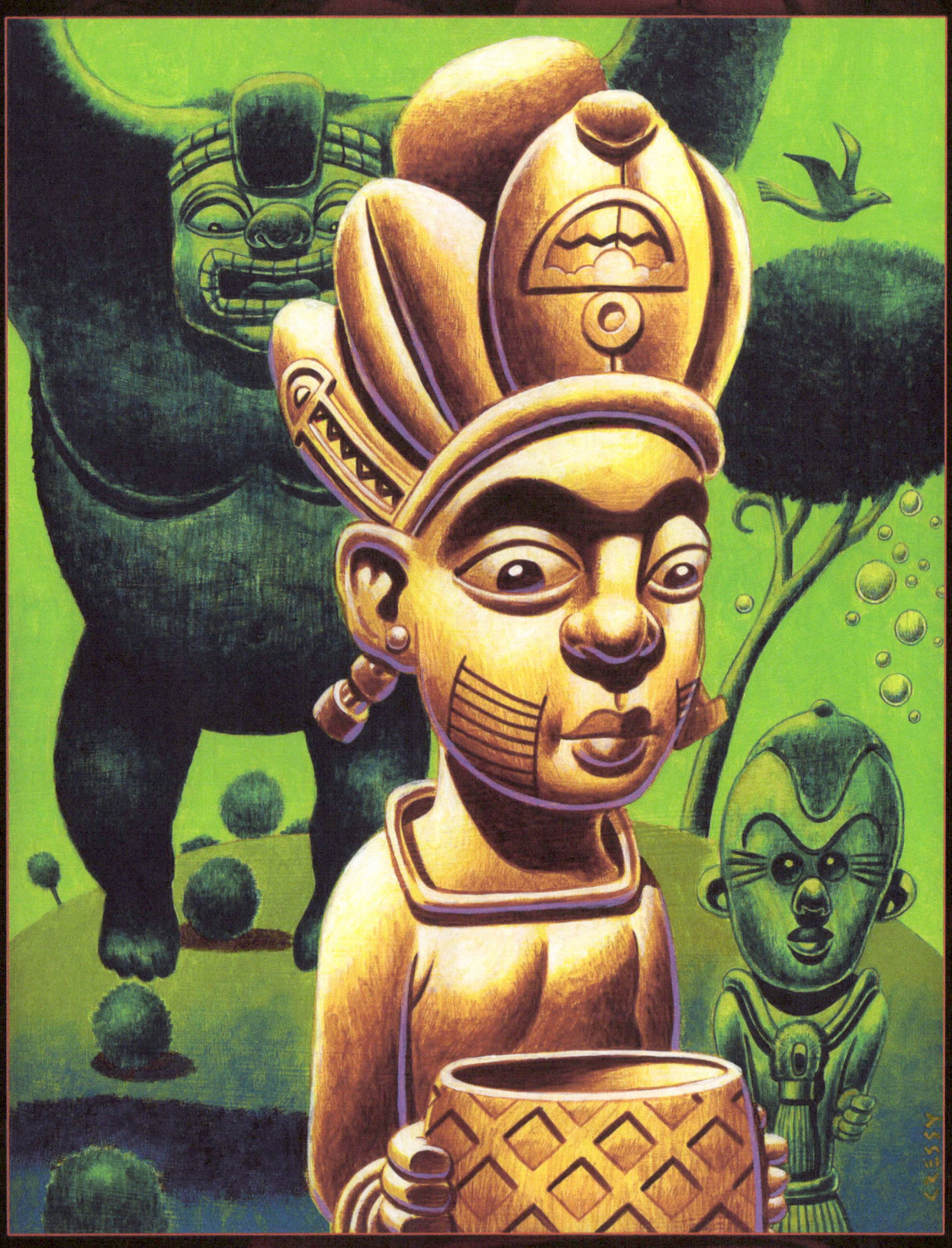

16" x 20" – Original Size

"Where your treasure is,
there will your heart be also"

"Bird Boy"

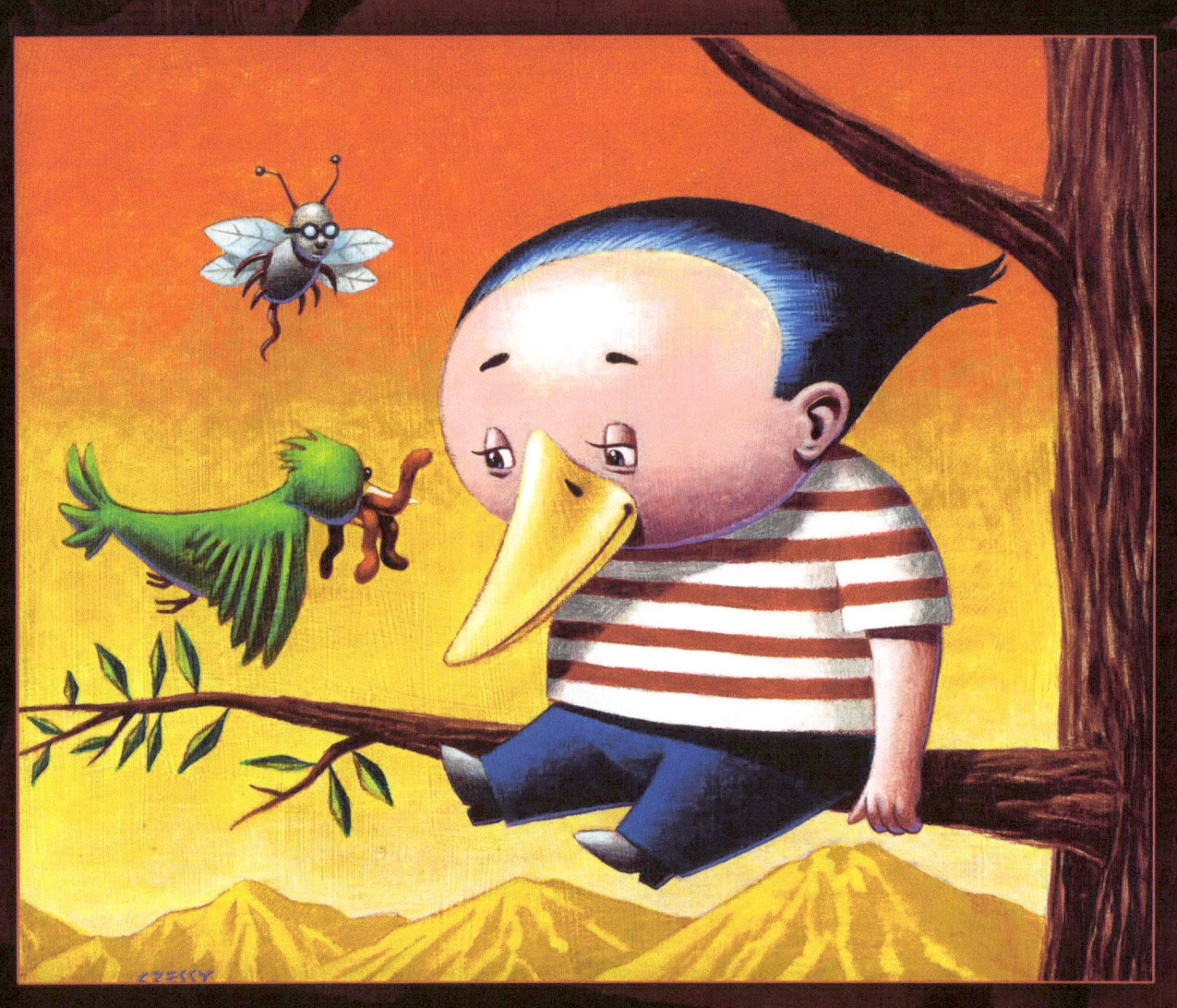

16" x 20" – Original Size

"A crab does not give birth to a bird"

"Family Drive"

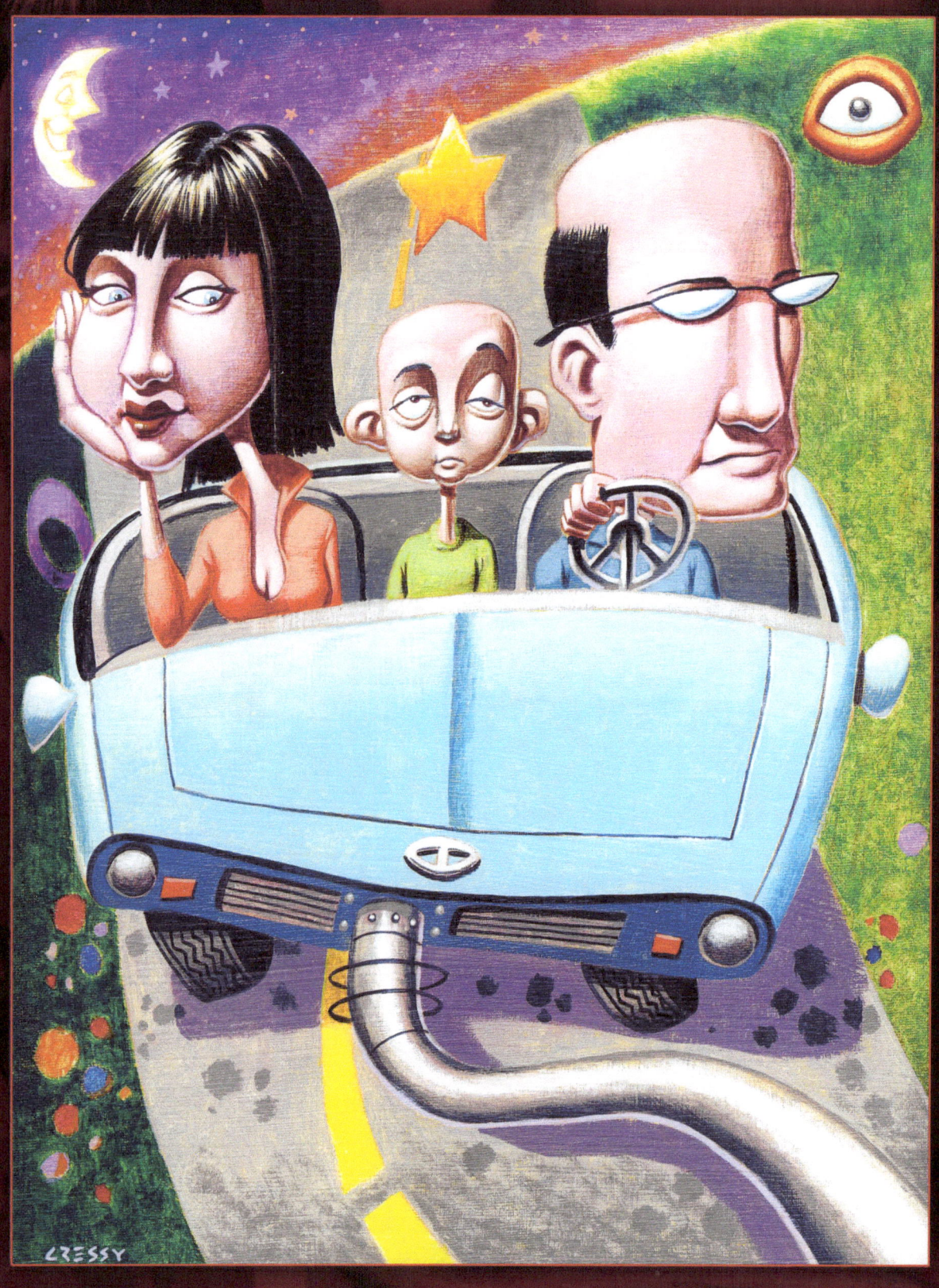

16" x 20" — Original Size

"In time of test, family is best"

"Bear Boys"

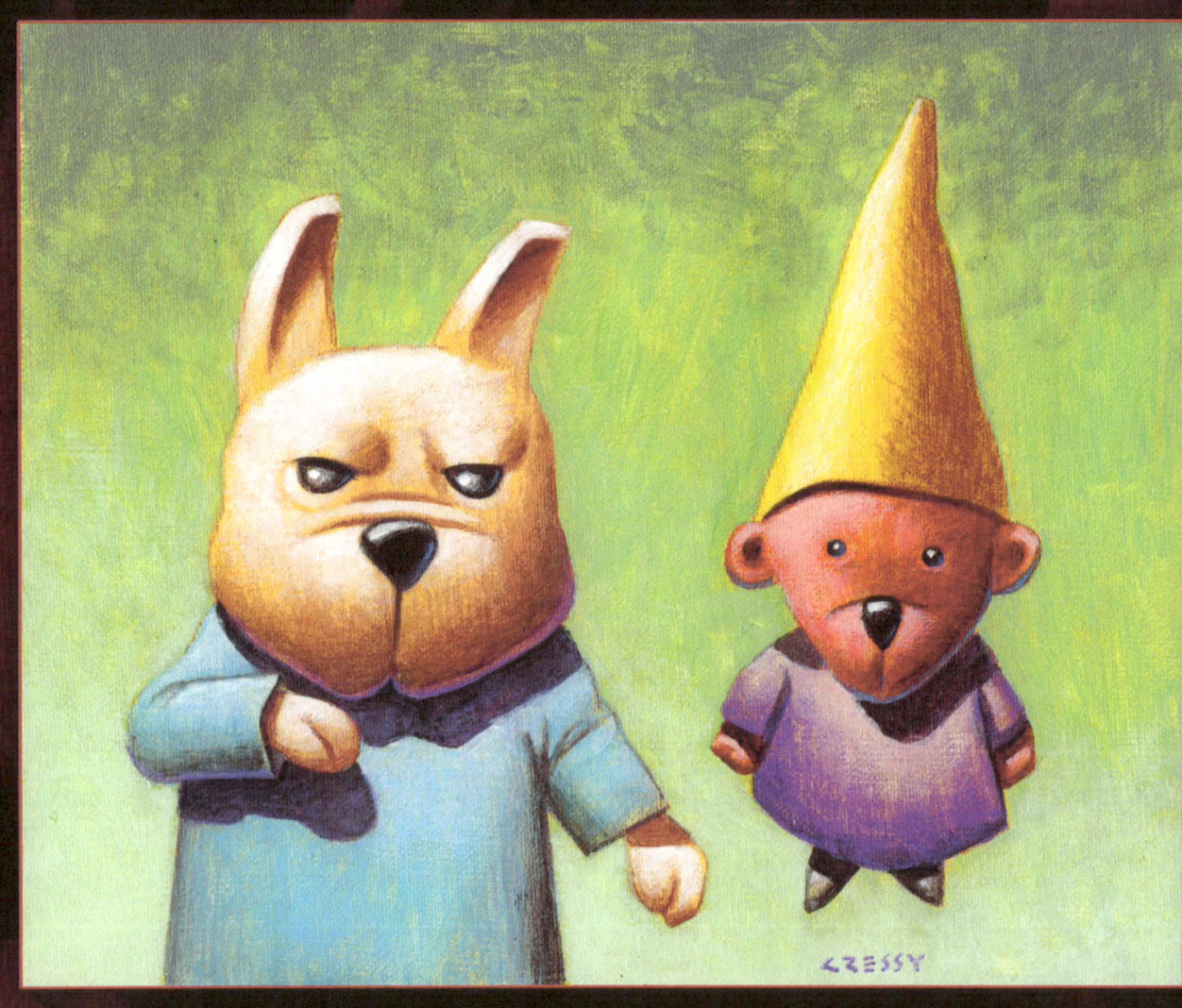

8" x 10" – Original Size

"Before you hibernate,
you're supposed to eat yourself stupid"

"Late Night Coffee Spot"

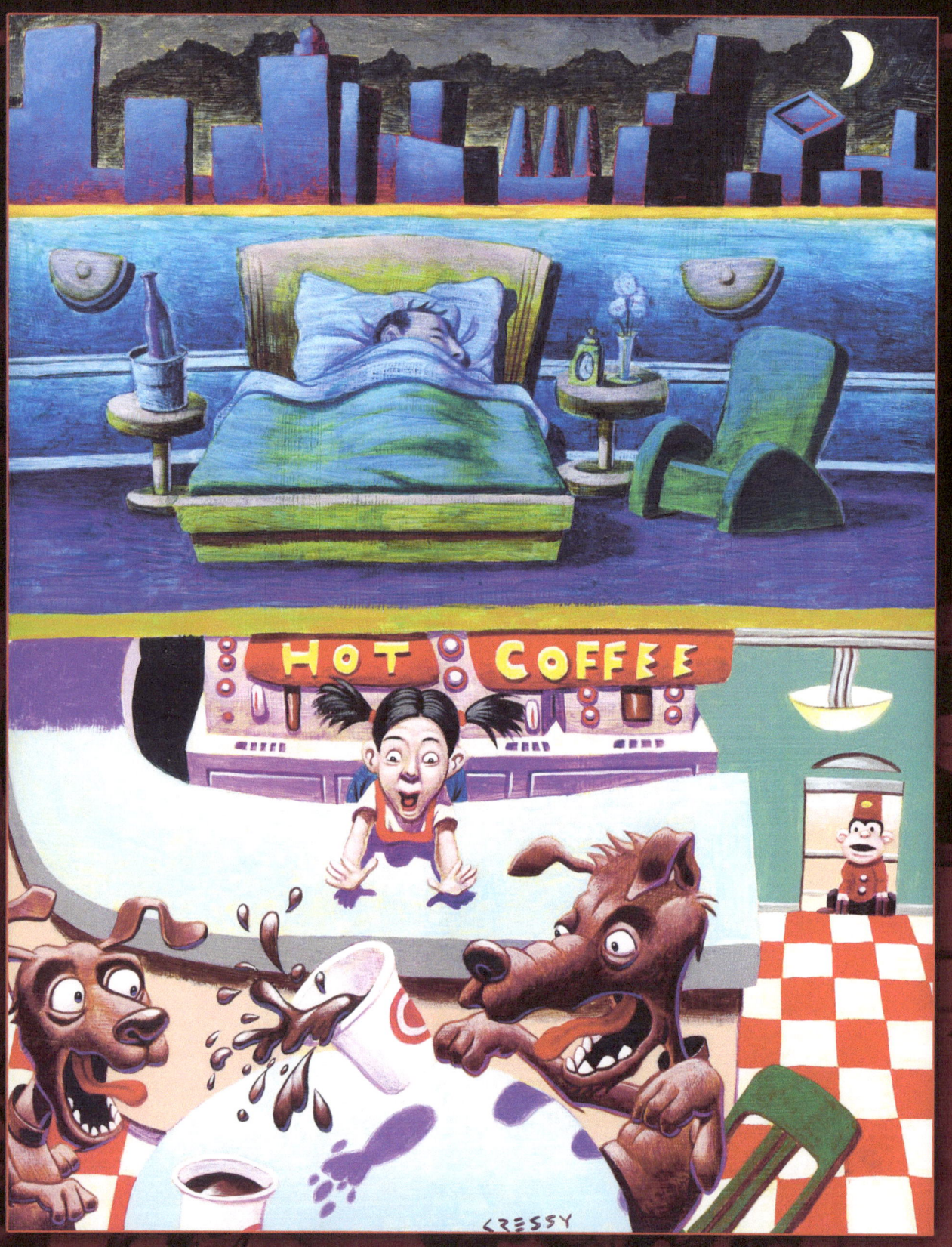

16" x 20" – Original Size

"Deja Brew:
The feeling that you've had this
coffee before"

"Memories of the Dollar"

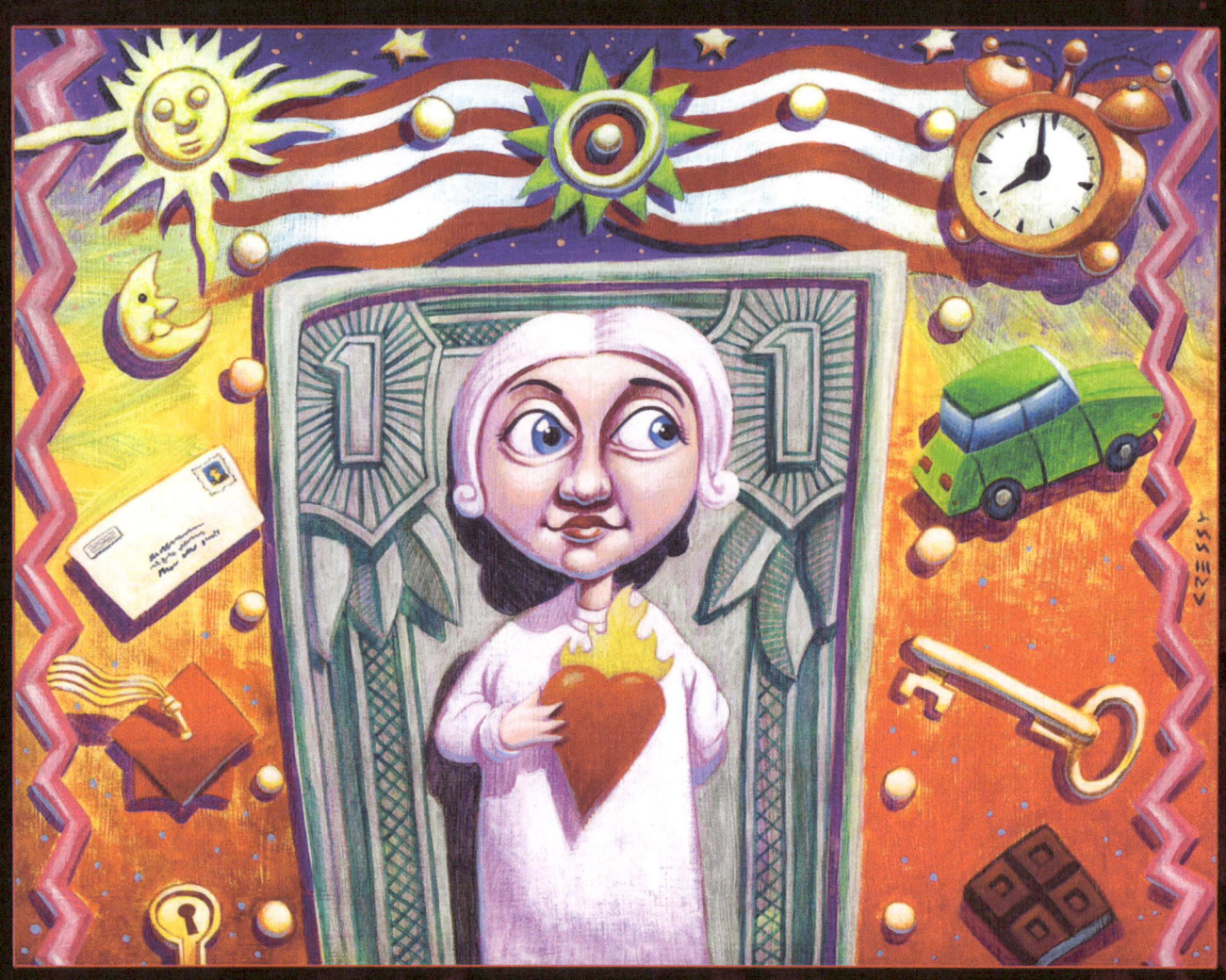

16" x 20" – Original Size

"Money can't buy happiness, but it can buy you the kind of misery you prefer"

"Cadet Trio"

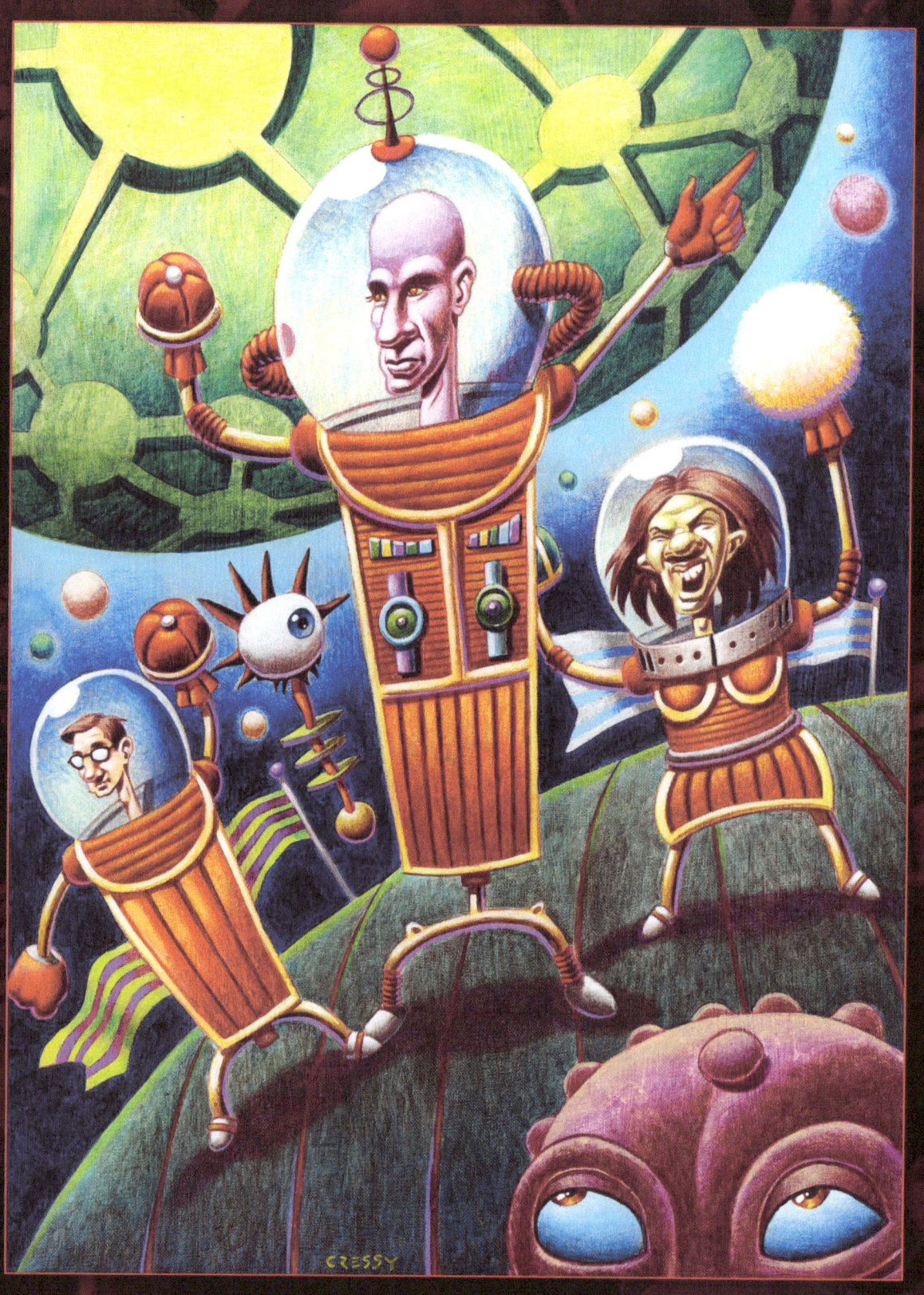

16" x 20" – Original Size

"Every leader needs to look back
once in a while to make sure
he has followers"

"The Duck"

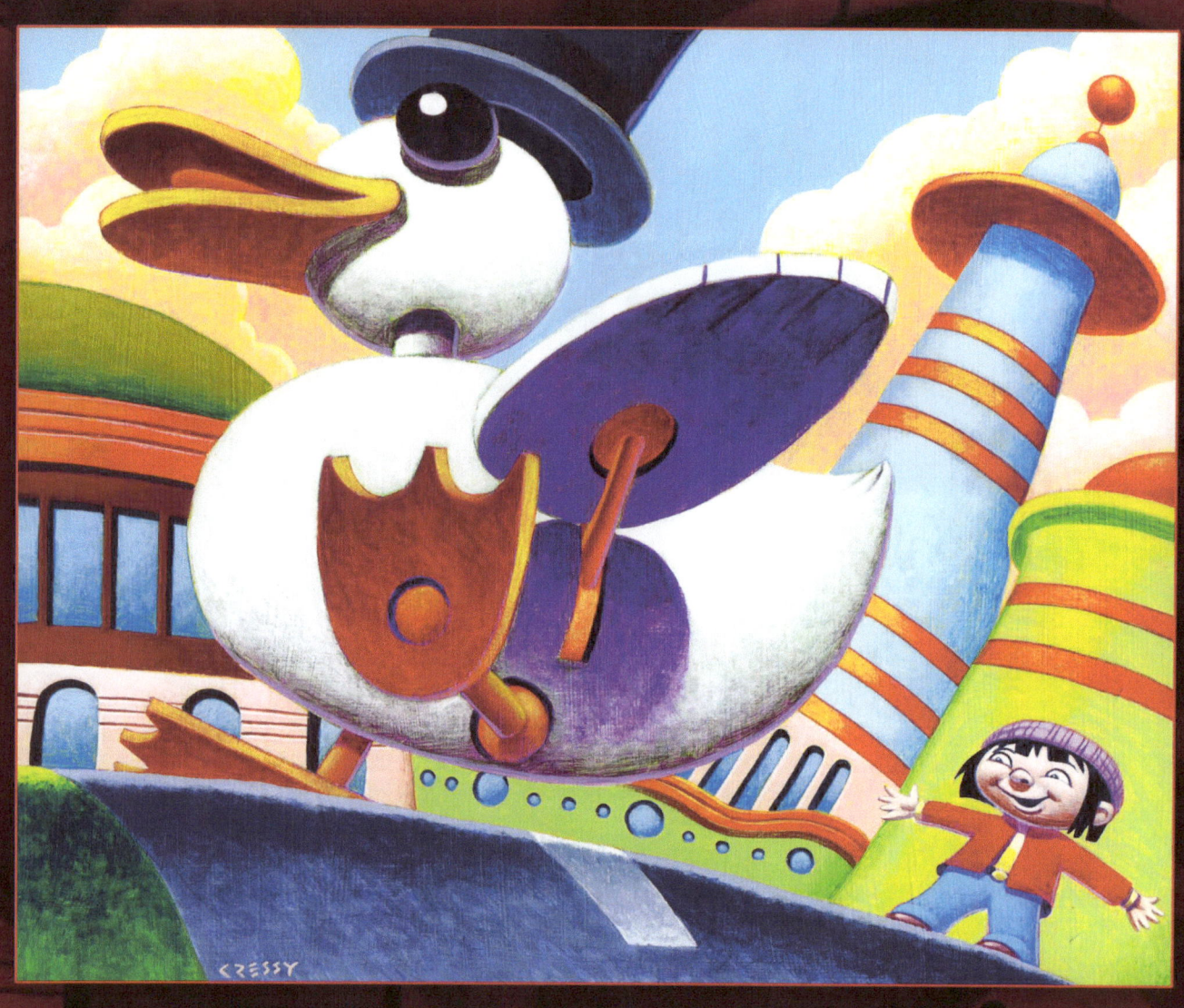

16" x 20" — Original Size

"When he walks he casts a shadow
of purpose"

"Chef's Bowl"

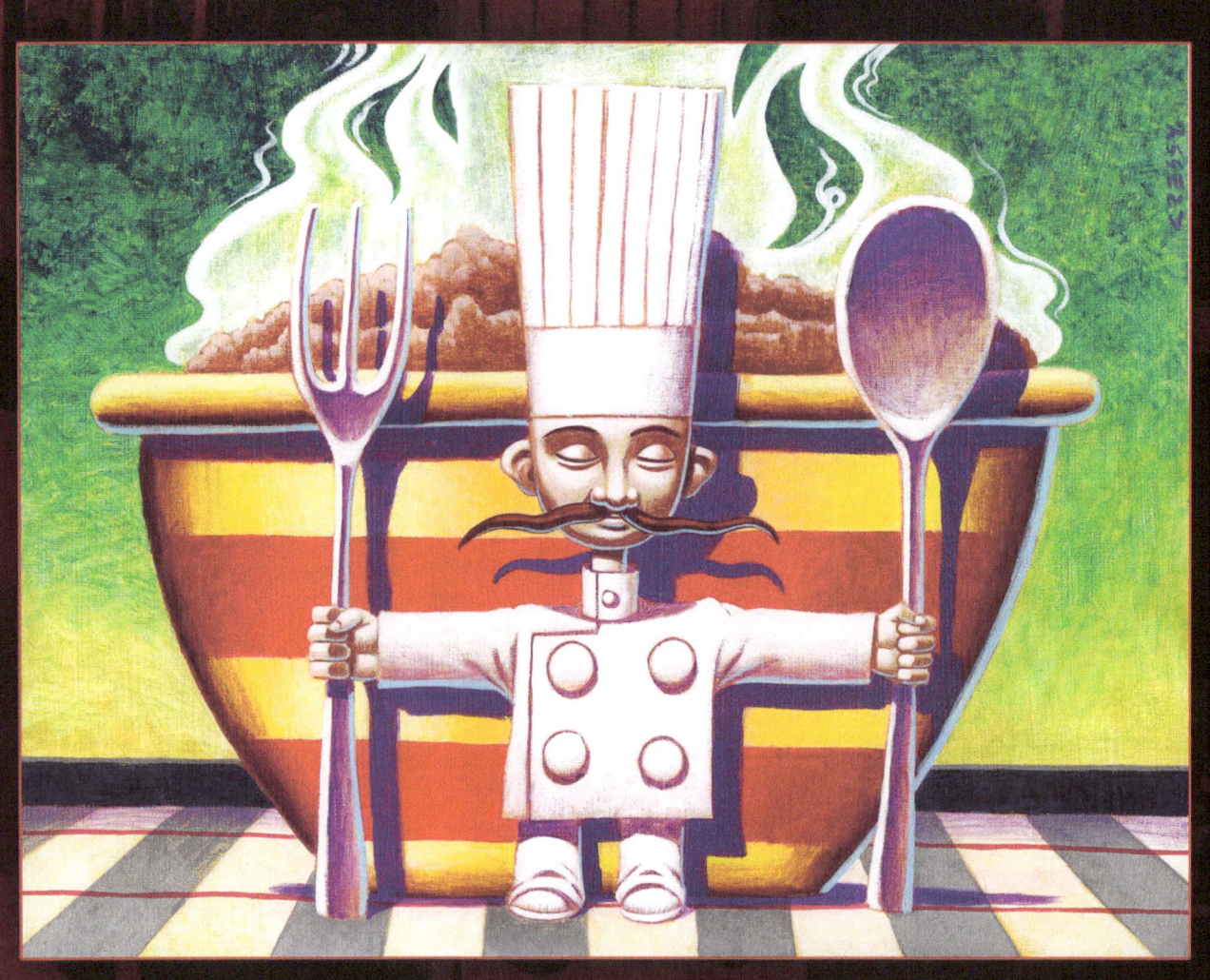

11" x 14" – Original Size

"Those who forget the pasta
are condemned to reheat it"

"Bright Guy in the Room"

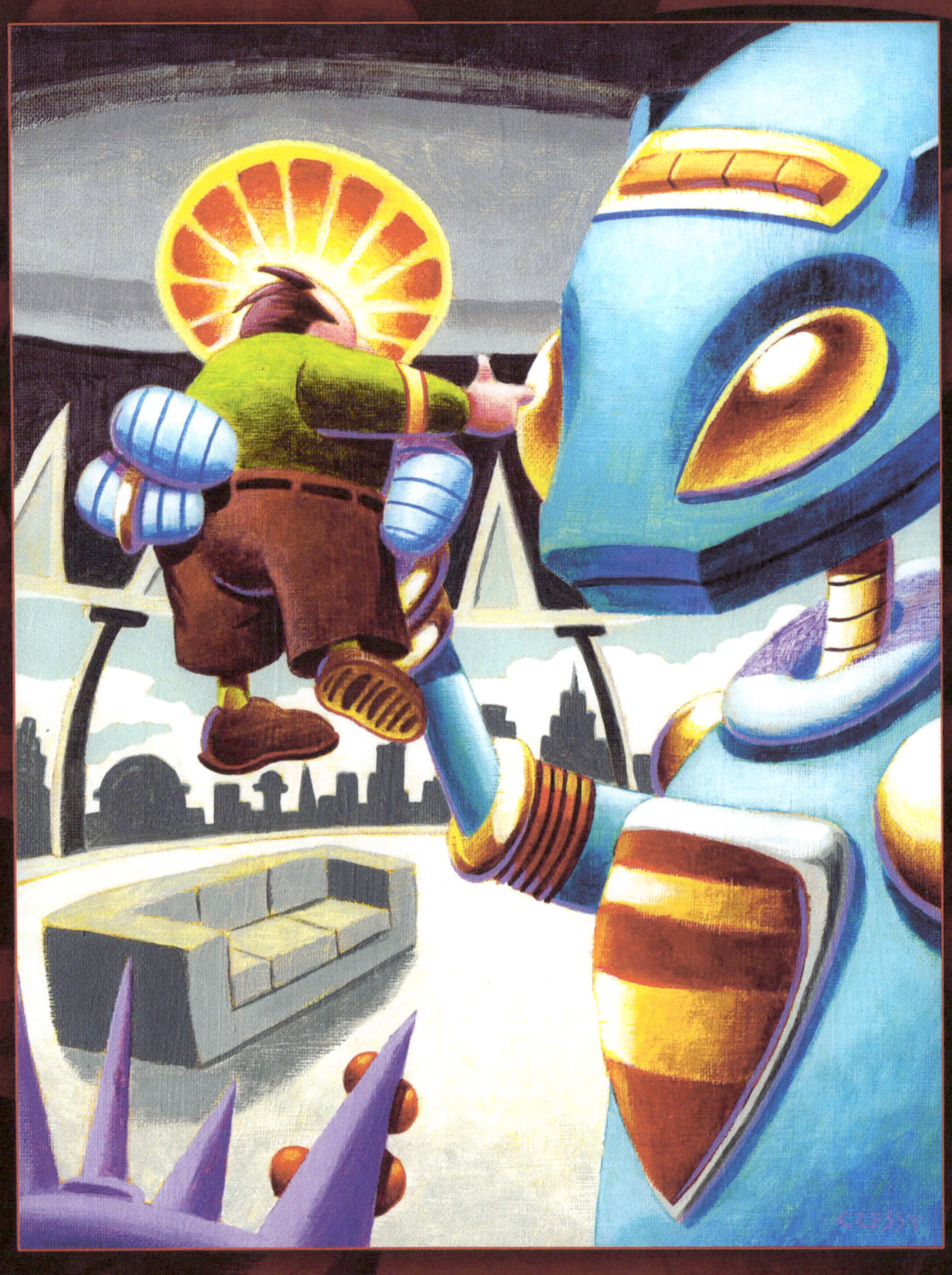

16" x 20" – Original Size

"There is no hope for a civilization
which starts each day to
the sound of an alarm clock"

"The Summer Wind"

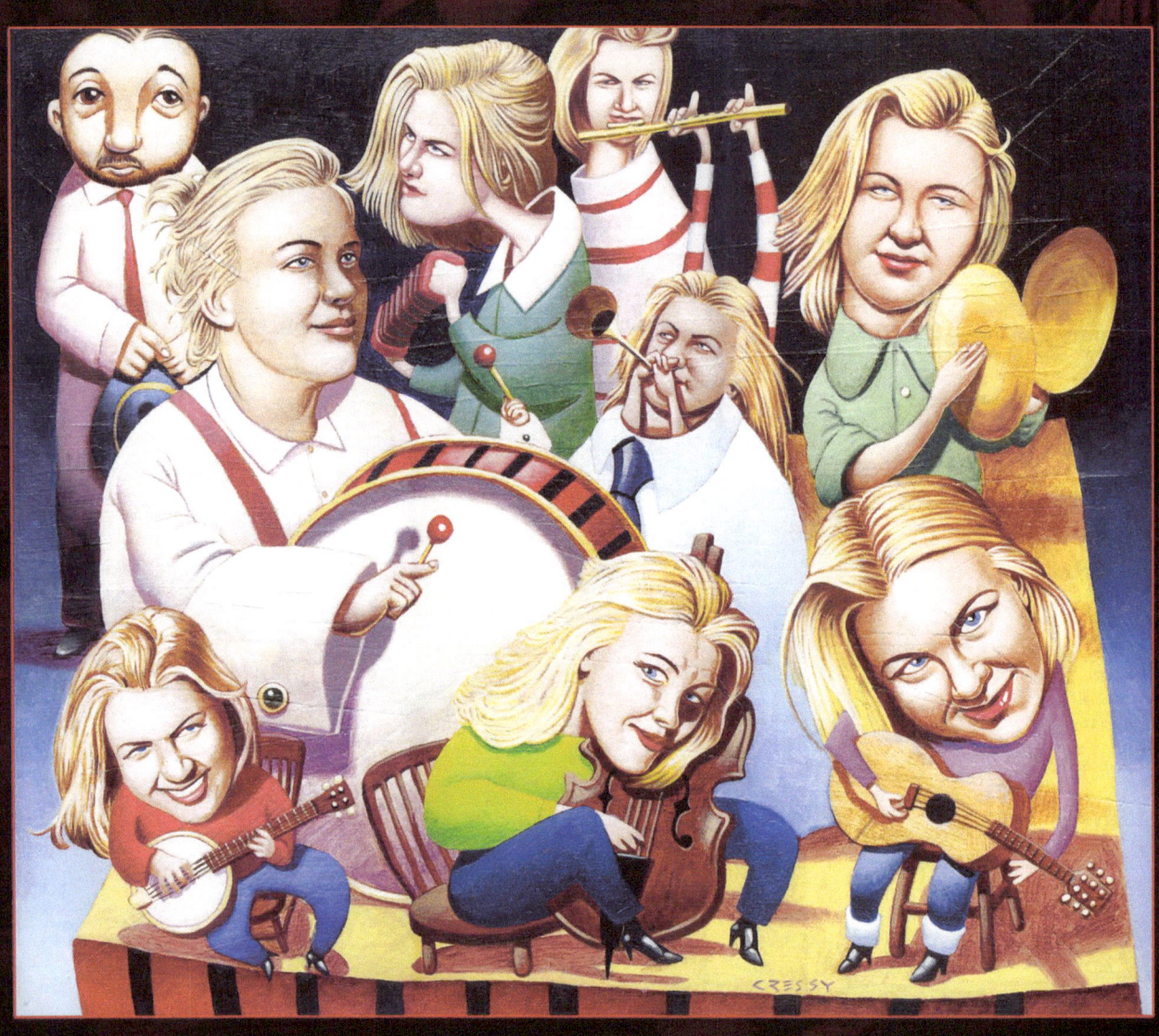

20" x 24" — Original Size

"We are all a little weird and life is a little weird, and when we find someone whose weirdness is compatible with ours, we join up with them and fall in mutual weirdness and call it love"

"Don Quixote and the Dragon"

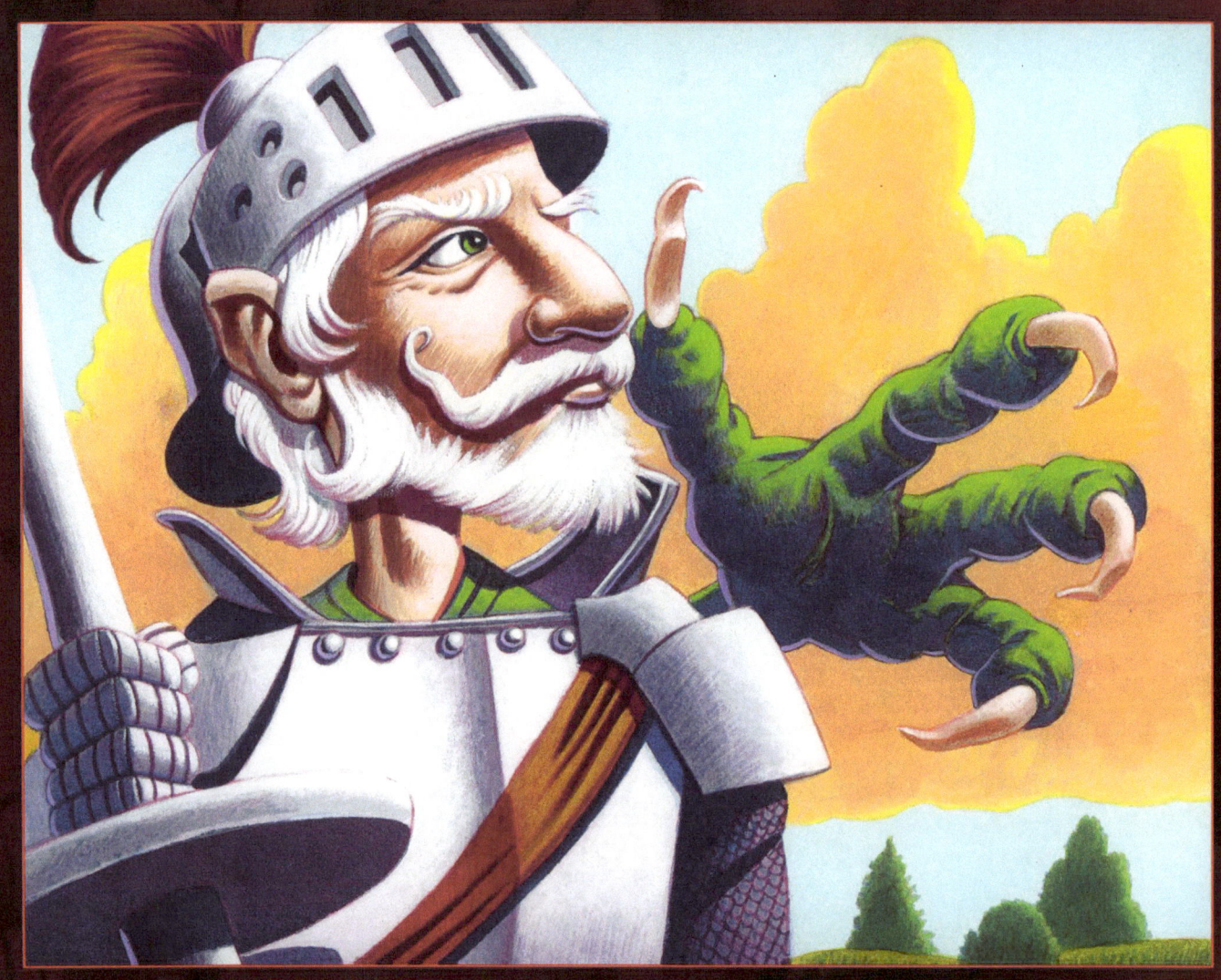

8" x 10" – Original Size

"Facts are the enemy of truth,
Everything else is artifice or illusion"

"Snail Candidate"

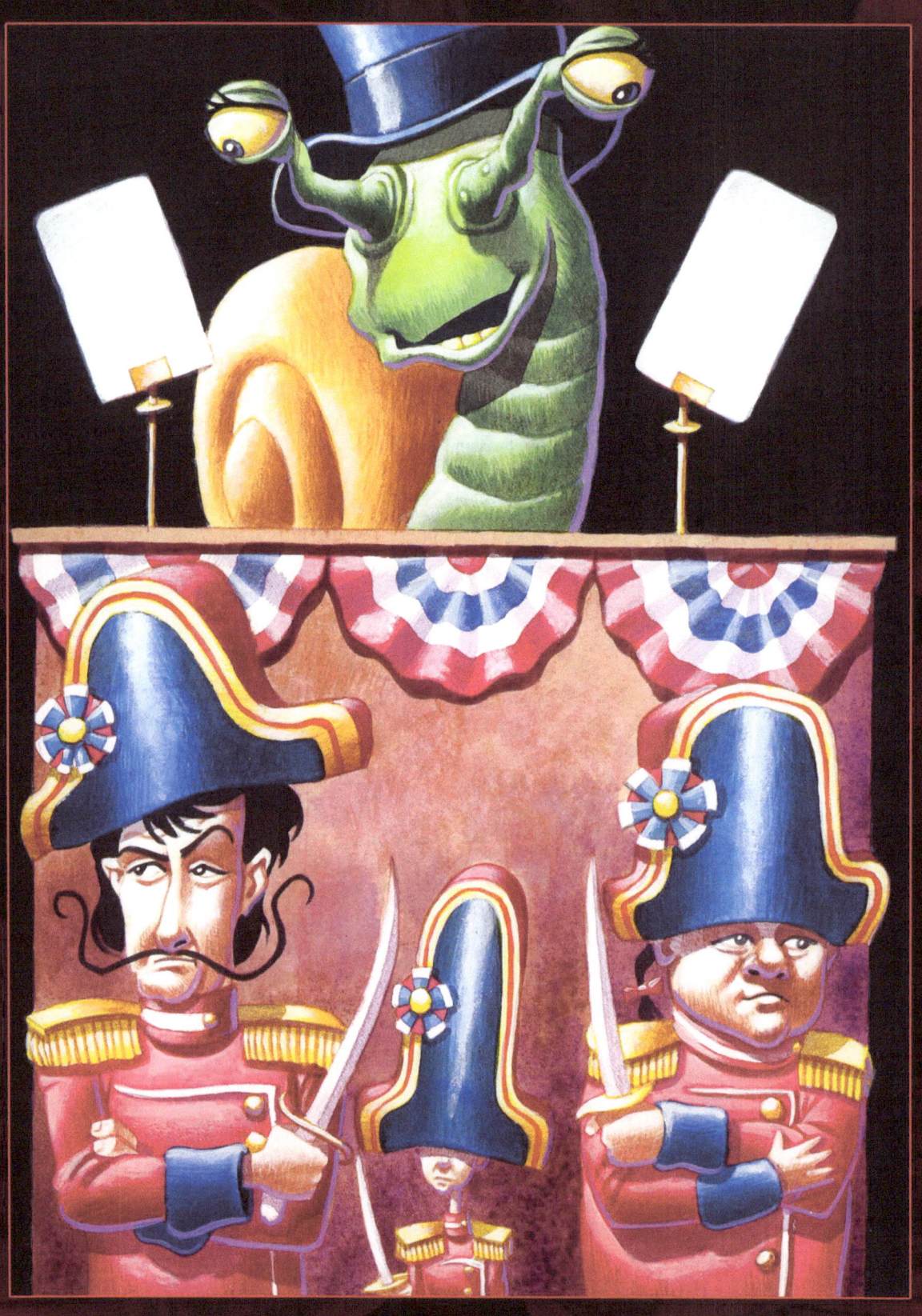

8" x 10" – Original Size

"We'd all like to vote for the best man, but he's never a candidate."

"Renaissance Robot"

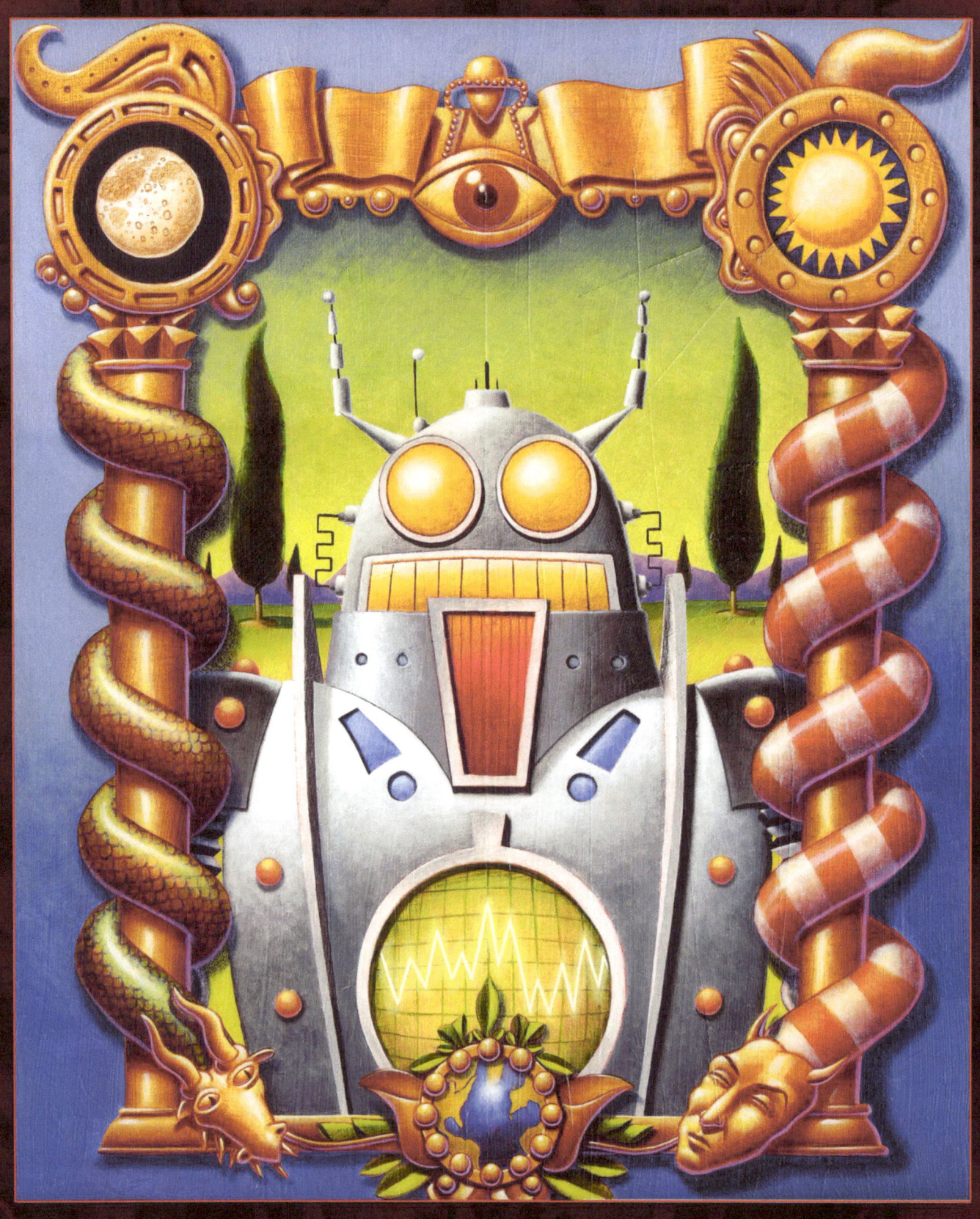

20" x 24" - Original Size

"All programmers are playwrights
and all computers are lousy actors."

"Boss Puppet"

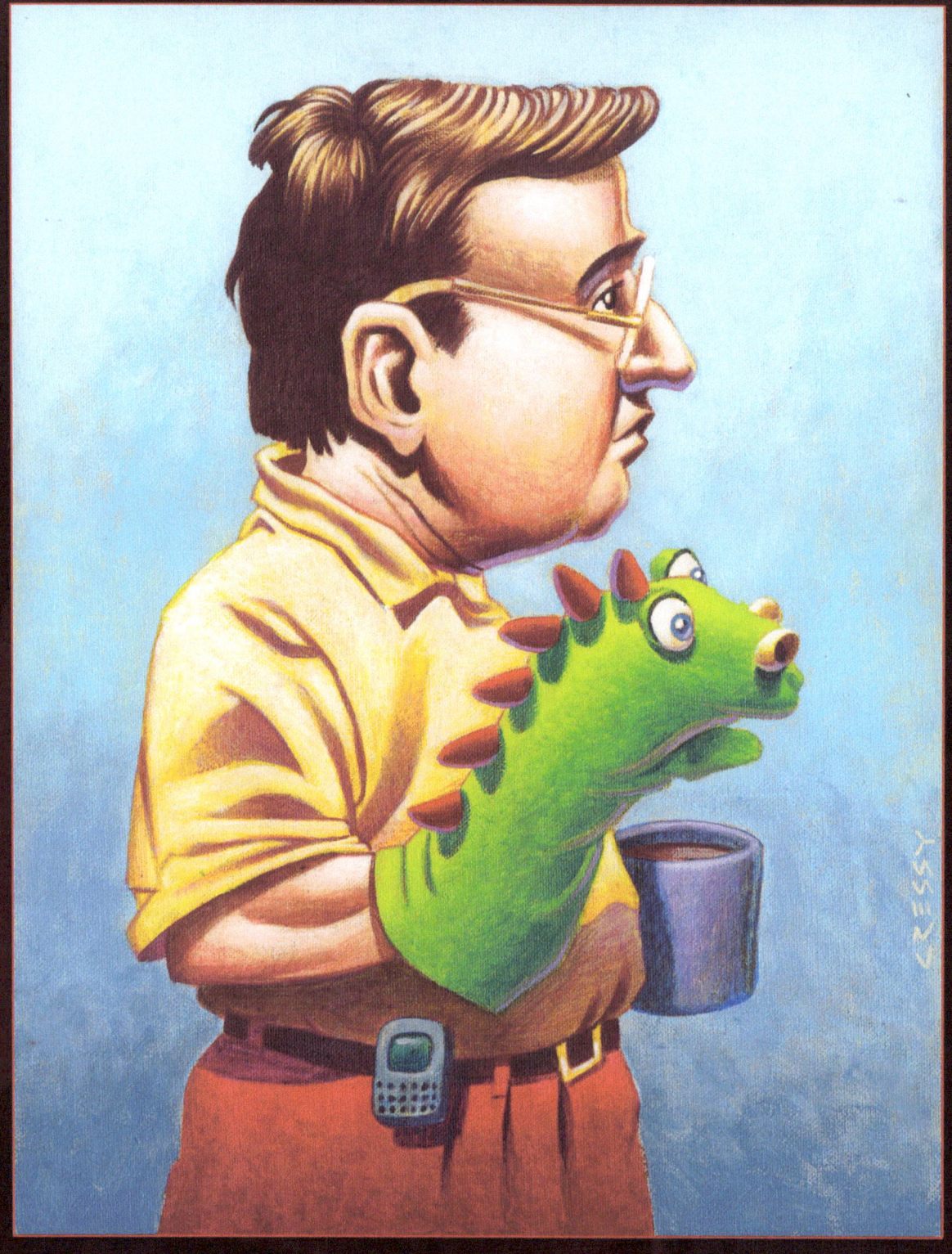

11" x 14" — Original Size

"Artificial Intelligence is no match
for natural stupidity"

ISBN 978-0-6152-0666-0